Some pages inside:
Branching Out Coloring Book Two

Welcome
Be
Creative
and
Happy
Coloring !
Be sure to place a sheet
of card stock behind
the page you are coloring when
using wet mediums!

Some pages inside:
Branching Out Coloring Book Two

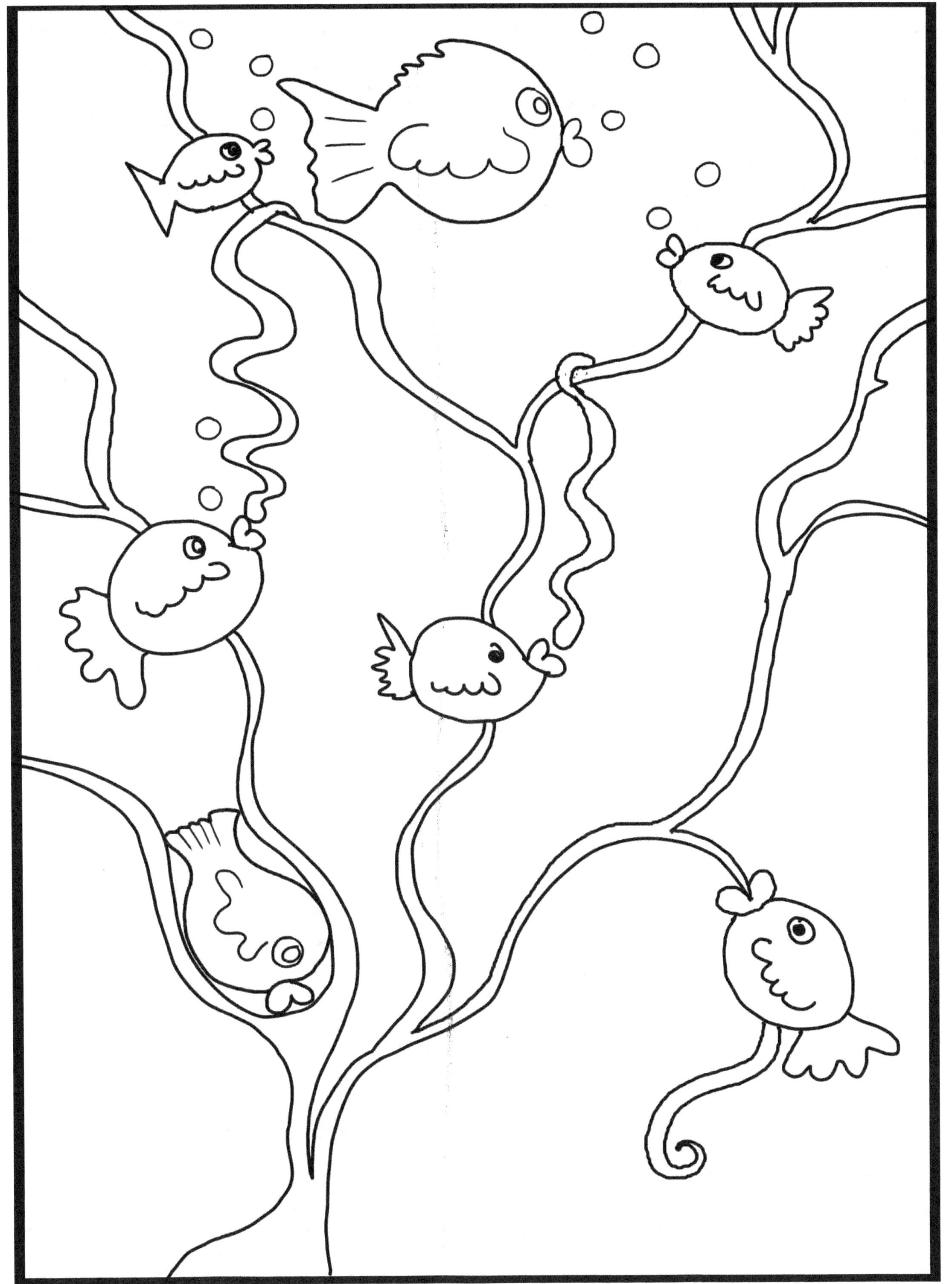

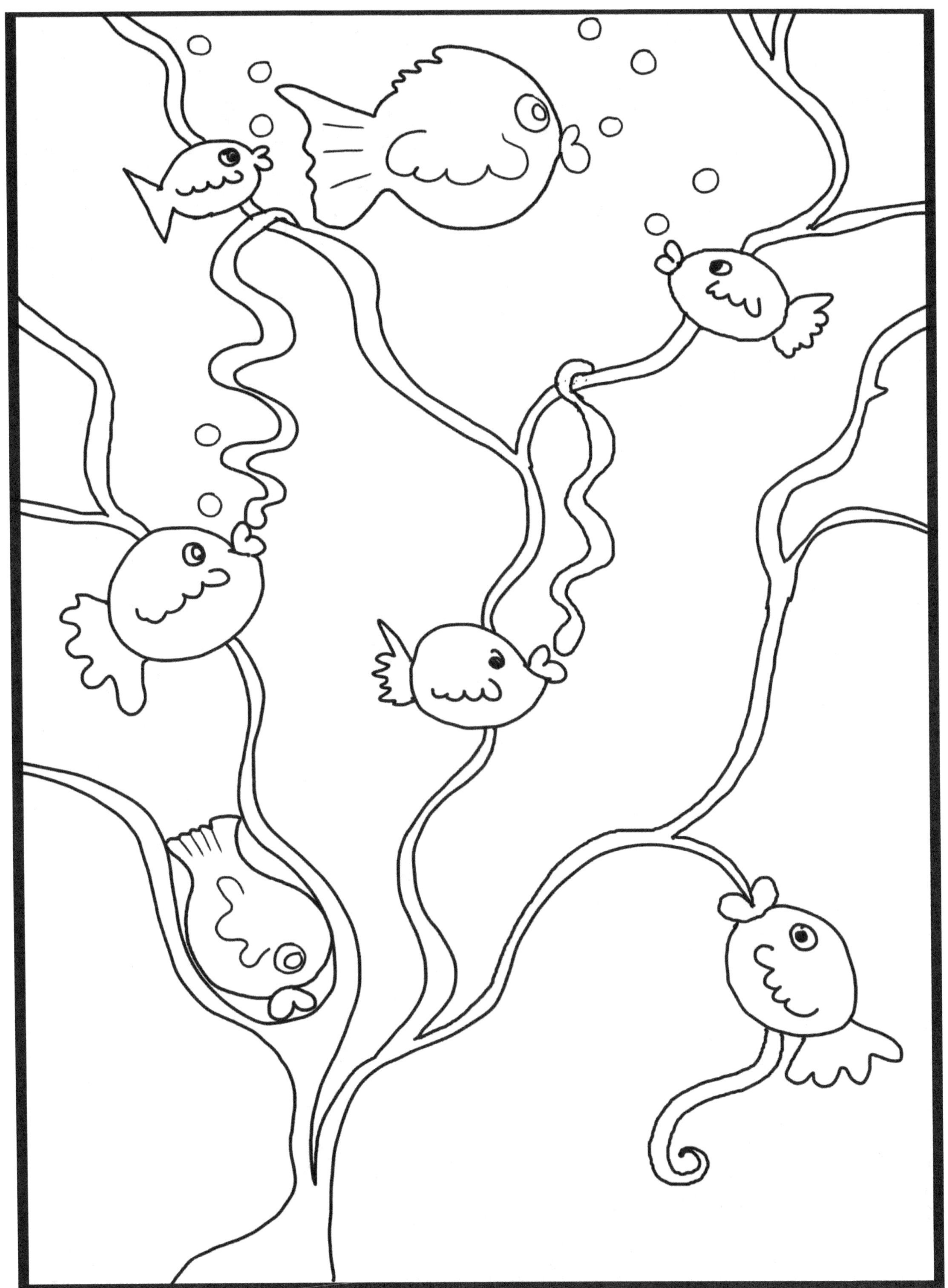

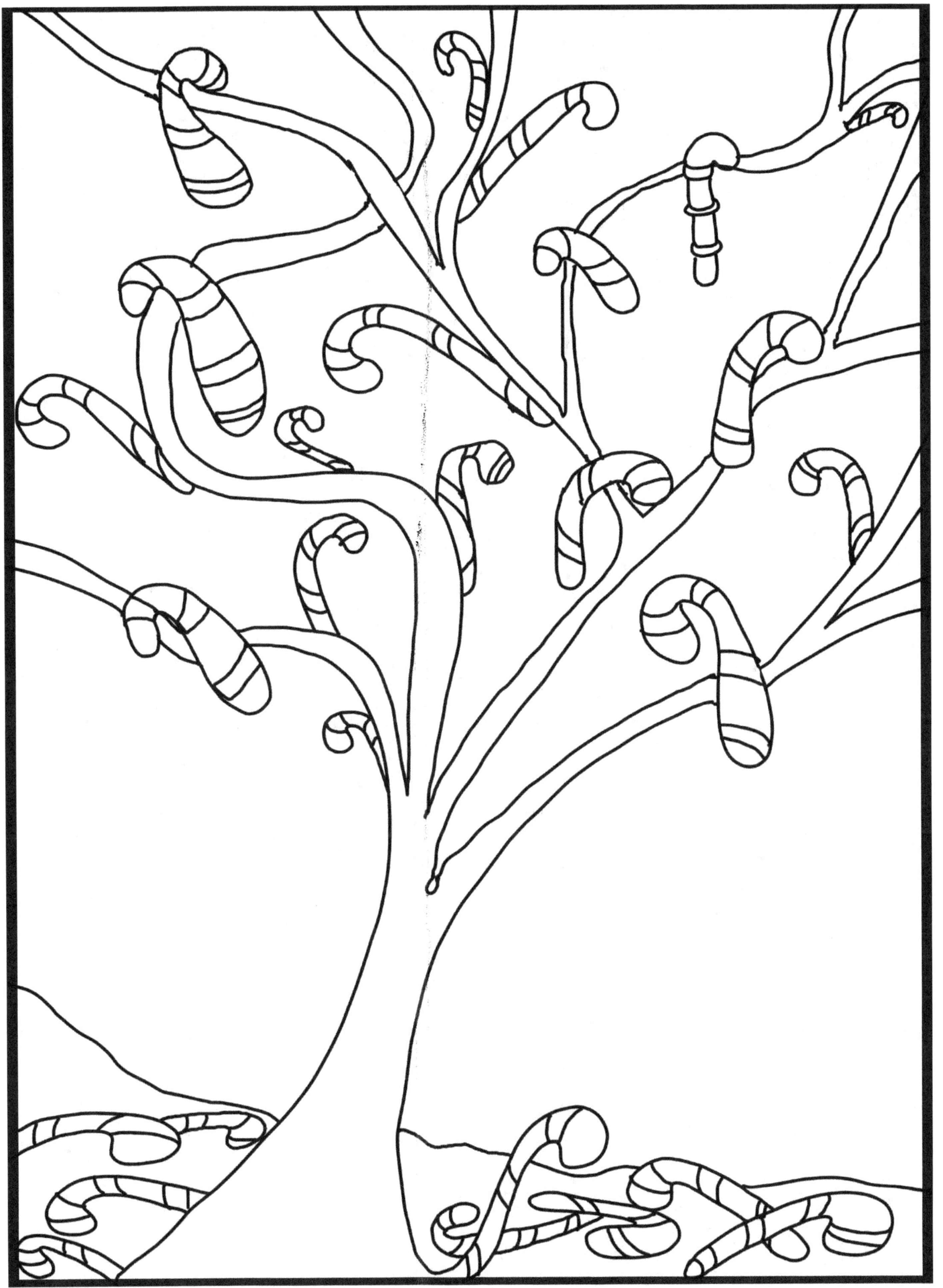

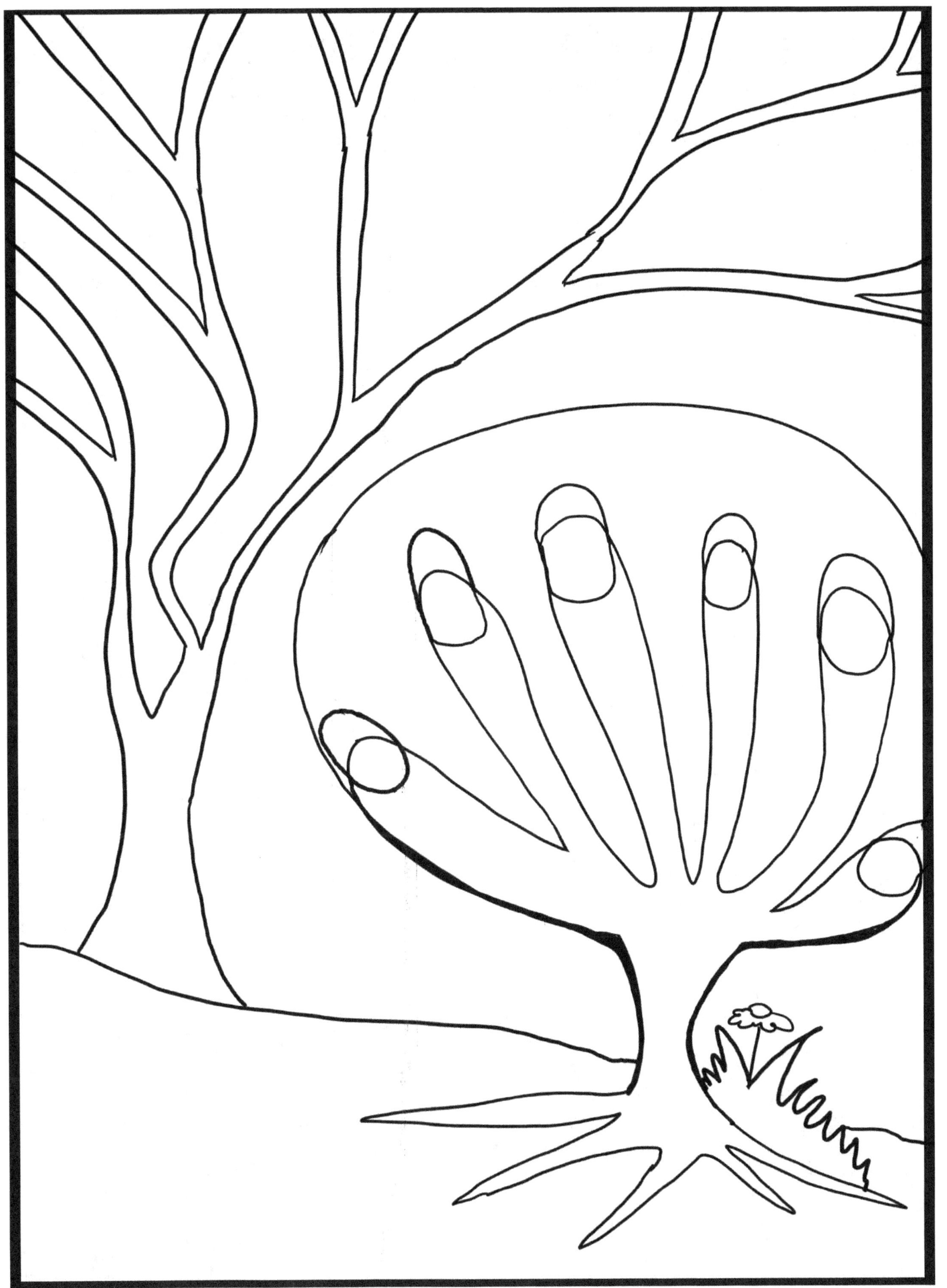

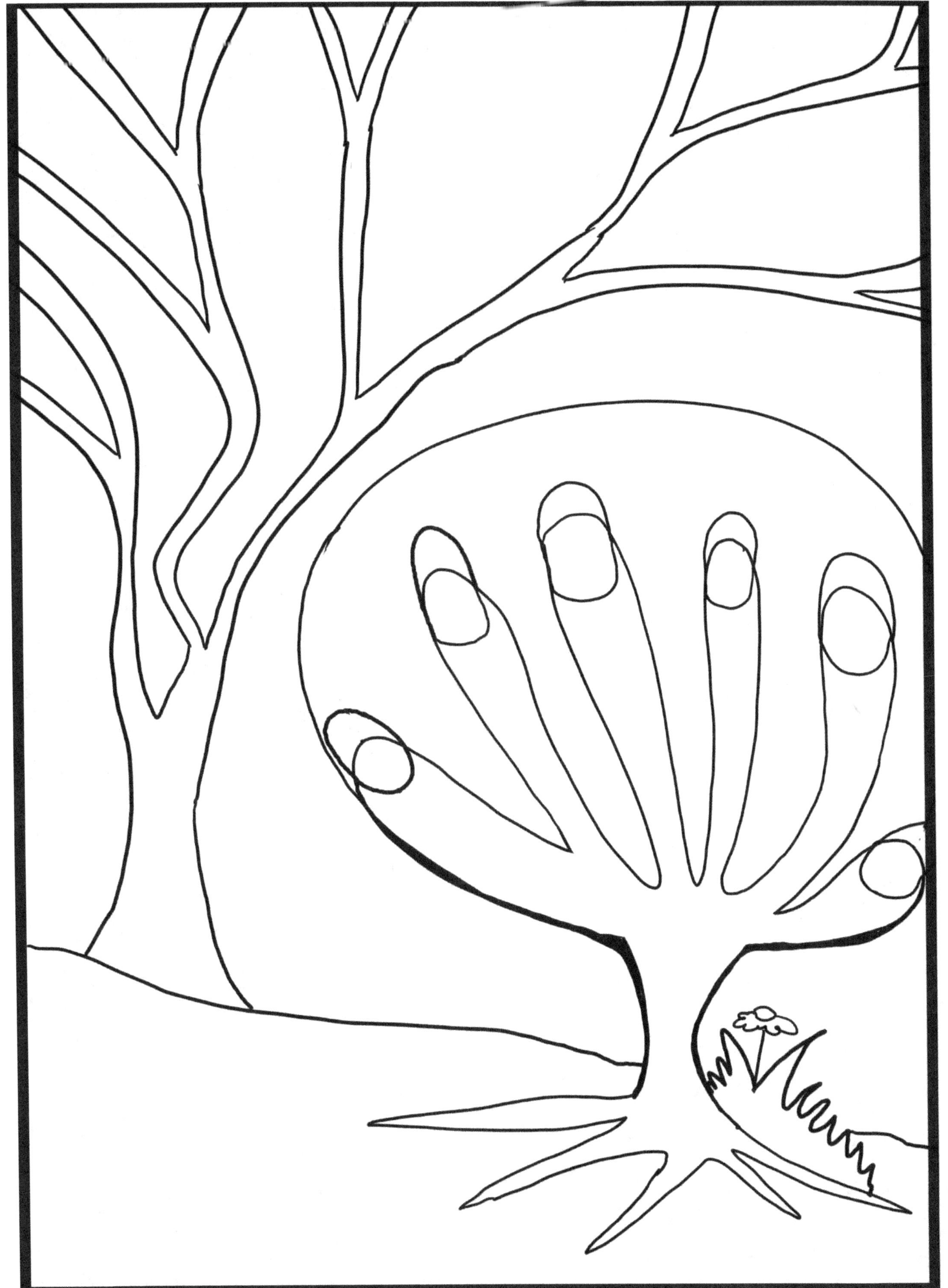

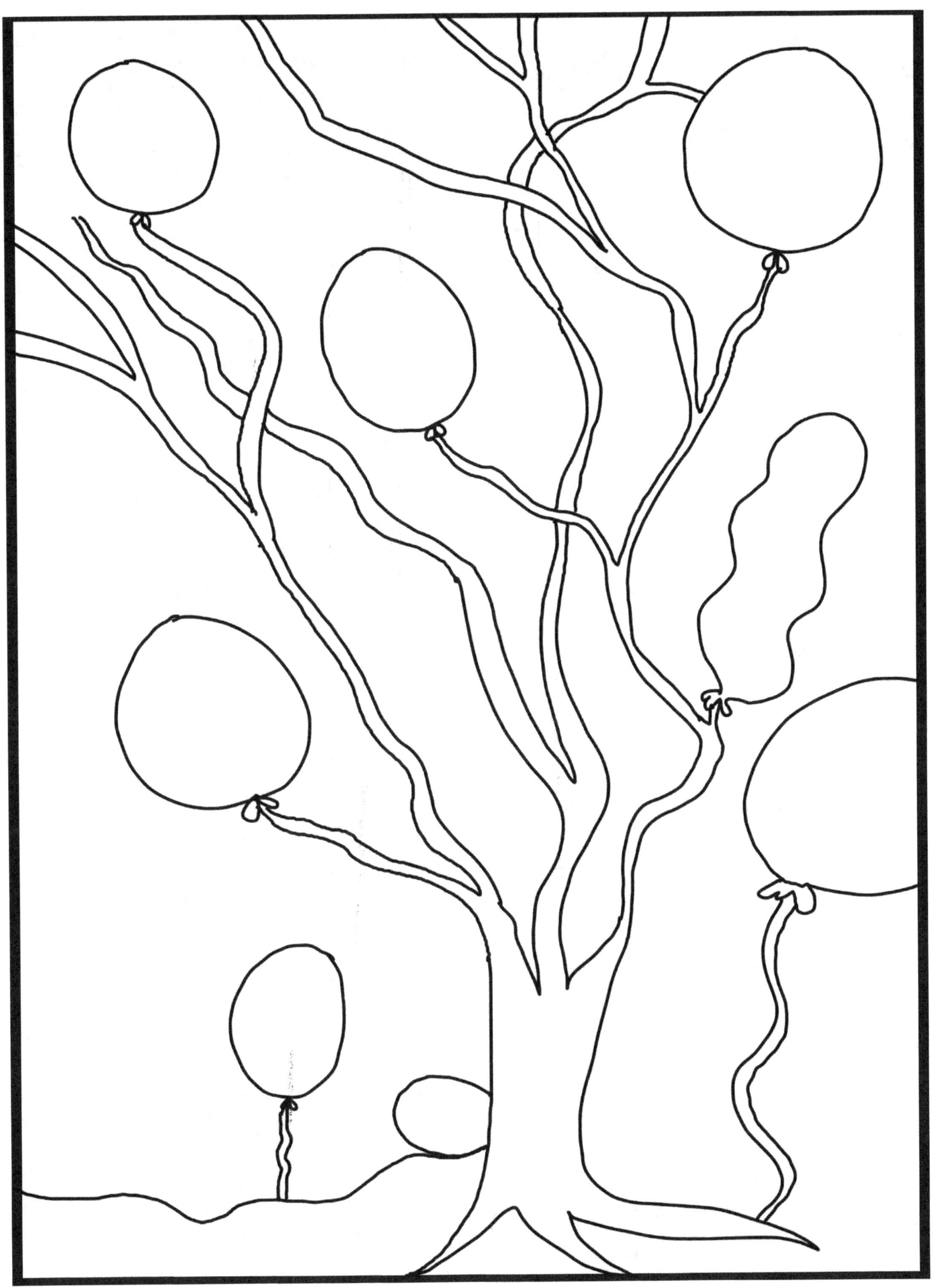

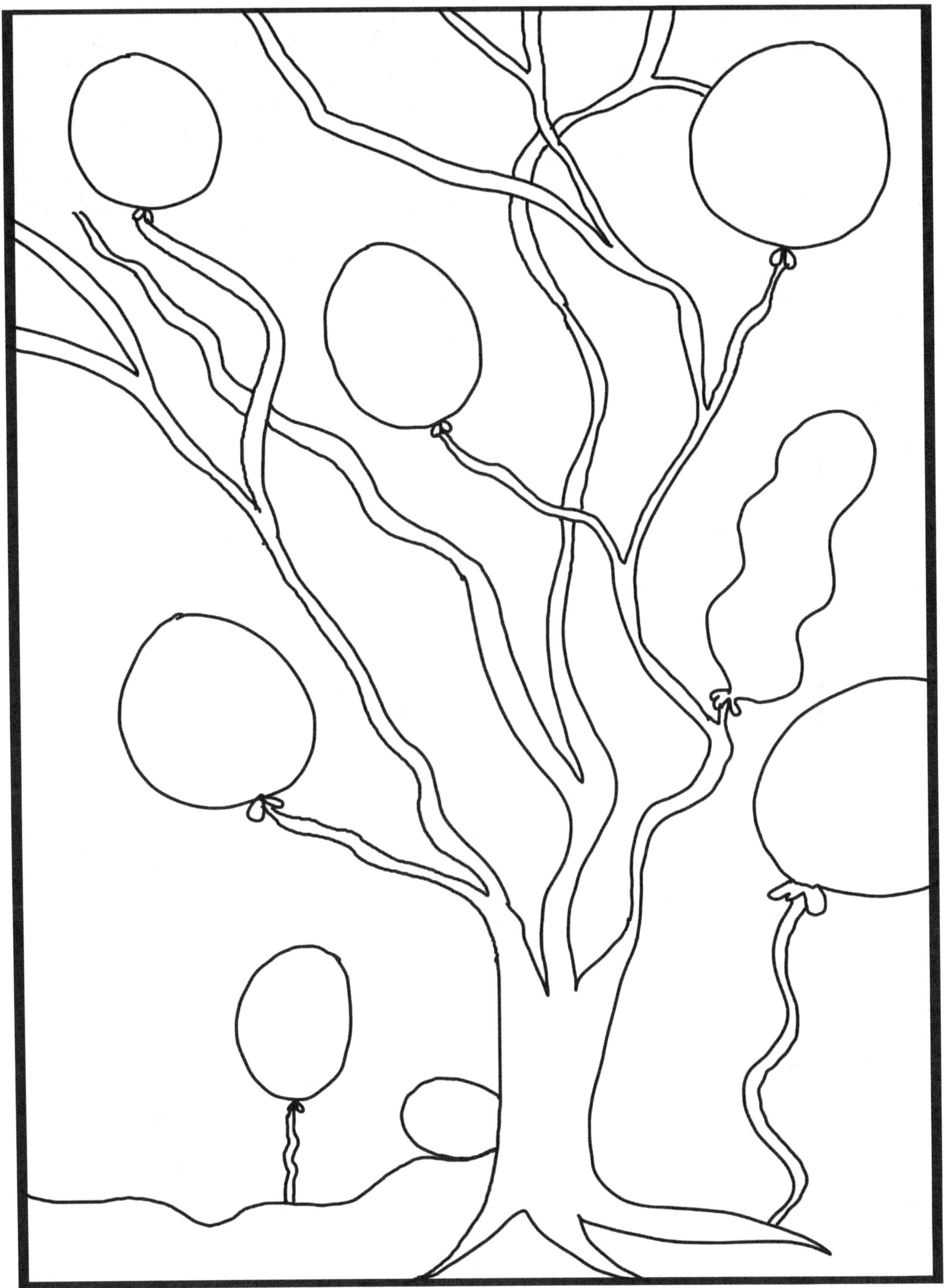

By:
Jill
Giannetta

By:
Jill
Giannetta

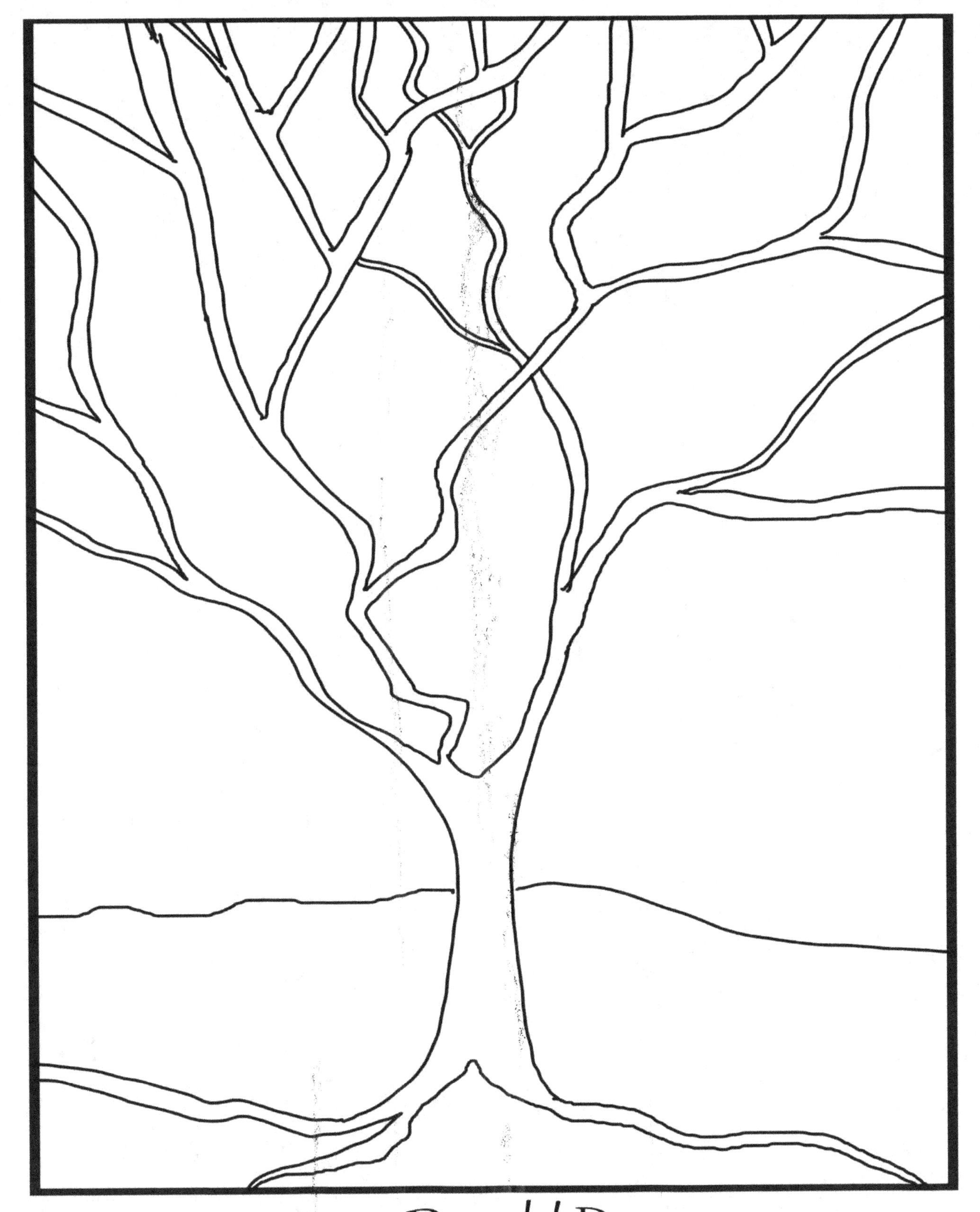

D. McDonald Designs

Branching Out Coloring Book Two

Created by: Rose Anthony

Branching Out Coloring Book Two

THIS

BOOK IS

ALL ABOUT

CREATIVITY

AND

FUN

WATCH WHAT DEB

DOES LIVE

ON FACEBOOK

WITH THESE

PAGES

All art is protected by

copyright laws

Deorah L. McDonald ©2019

FIND
DEBORAH L. MCDONALD
ON
FACEBOOK
D.MCDONALD DESIGNS
COLORING CLUB
TO SEE PAGE
BY PAGE FLIP THRU
TOURS..... JUST ASK,
SOME GOOD PERSON
WILL DIRECT YOU
TO WHERE!

Please
Be
Kind
and
Return
to
Amazon
and
give this
book
some
stars
and a review
and perhaps
share a few pages
you colored!
Thanks!
J. McDonald

d. mcdonald designs

Fabulous Florals Two

D.McDonald Designs
Home Tweet Home

Stained Glass Coloring Book
For Adults and Gifted Children
Deborah L Mc Donald......Amazon

Stained Glass Coloring Book Two
For Adults and Gifted Children

Deb's Fun Furnishings Adult Coloring Book

This book covers special days in the year with coloring pages and cards along with bonus pages from the Dark Hearts Collection

Stained Glass Coloring Book Two
For Adults and Gifted Children

D. McDonald Designs
Sunflowers & Sayings
Adult Coloring Book

D. McDonald Designs
Sunflowers & Sayings
Adult Coloring Book